KU-061-301

We have been giving the Giles annual to my father at Christmas for the past thirty five years. He invariably receives it with the same amazed cry: 'Giles! How splendid'. He knows it's as much for all the family as it is for him.

What I love best about Giles' work is the way he marries the stupendously drawn backdrops with the cartoon characters which occupy centre stage. With the long-perfected skill of the animator, he shows that two quite separate styles of drawing thrive one on top of the other.

From Giles' backdrops I have developed a passion for his England in summertime: hot empty suburban streets shadowed by wonderfully drawn trees; sodden cricket pitches, fly-ridden picnics and seedy boarding houses. Giles draws winters like no-one else, thick snow settling on ledges and railways, dark skies over rain-lashed harbours and empty railway stations, Whitehall in a blizzard. Hordes of people have come to life through Giles' pen, each one a complete individual drawn with acute observation. Distant figures are treated in extravagant detail, and all his pictures reward closer scrutiny.

The Giles family is now legendary: Mother bogged down with the housework, Vera's dripping nose, Dad's laconic asides, anarchic children, baleful dogs filching food and the immortal Grandma, mouth snapped shut like a turtle, coal-sack body clutching padlocked handbag. She and the skull-headed Chalkie are my favourites (as children we used to practice doing Chalkie's cadaverous leer), but I have a special affection for George Junior, the anxious ping-pong ball of a baby to whom all manner of dreadful things happen.

Salutations, great Giles! and thank you for another year of your incomparable wit and artistic genius.

warmest good wishes

Joanna Lumley

"Perhaps this'll teach you to stay at 'ome next 'oliday."

Sunday Express, April 9th, 1944

SUNDAY EXPRESS & DAILY EXPRESS
CARTOONS

FORTY-SEVENTH SERIES

BOOKS

Published by Pedigree Books Limited
The Old Rectory, Matford Lane, Exeter, Devon, EX2 4PS.
Under licence from Express Newspapers plc.
Printed in Italy. © 1993 Express Newspapers plc.

£3.95

Gl 47

INTRODUCTION

by

JOANNA

LUMLEY

"There 'e goes—says he's going to get this ruddy invasion over, then get some leave."

Sunday Express, May 14th, 1944

"This happens to me every day since the invasion started."

Sunday Express, July 2nd, 1944

"Now I want you to promise me you're all going to be really *good* little evacuees and not worry his Lordship."

Sunday Express, July 30th, 1944

"Are you addressing ME?"

Daily Express, Oct. 8th, 1944

"I don't care if you *are* supposed to be Marshal Koniev—you're not playing Warsaw in my yard."

Sunday Express, Jan. 21st, 1945

"I bet you think it funny that a bloke like me can choose wot Government I like."

Daily Express, May 23rd, 1945

"Got any good tips for the dogs tonight, chum?"

Sunday Express, Nov. 11th, 1945

"Now which of you beauties is going to volunteer to be Father Christmas for the platoon tomorrow night?"

Sunday Express, Dec. 23rd, 1945

"Now, boys, it is not only on our great statesmen that the future of the world depends, it is you—who are about to take your place as responsible citizens, etc., etc. . . . ."

Sunday Express, Jan. 13th, 1946

"If you don't quit whistling 'Your tiny hand is frozen' I'm going to come over and do yer."

Daily Express, Mar. 5th, 1946

"I suppose you've read that you can now be fined up to £5,000 and get seven years for doing unessential building."

Sunday Express, Mar. 24th, 1946

"And if the world isn't blown up by atom bomb tests before I get my demob. we'll get married—if we can get a house."

Daily Express, Mar. 28th, 1946

"If they did away with wars there'd be no need for Victory Parades."

Sunday Express, June 9th, 1946

"It's me husband, Sir—he won't come out. Says he's had about all he can stand of the outside world."

Sunday Express, Sept. 8th, 1946

"This go-slow strike'll shake the people who thought British railways couldn't go any slower."

Sunday Express, Nov. 24th, 1946

"And now here is a jolly quiz for everybody to join in. Have you all got your pencils and little pieces of paper ready?"

Sunday Express, Dec. 1st, 1946

"Bright idea of yours—taking them to the circus—wasn't it?"

Sunday Express, Dec. 29th, 1946

"I'll laugh if there's no —— lines under this lot."

Daily Express, Feb. 6th, 1947

"Why couldn't they wait till after Christmas before they told them about this no Christmas box business?"

Daily Express, Dec. 16th, 1947

"More stealing than ever this Christmas—they'd have your blooming trousers if you didn't watch 'em."

Daily Express, Dec. 18th, 1947

"Give it up, George. Christmas is over now, anyway."

Sunday Express, Dec. 28th, 1947

"A husband is entitled to chastise his wife provided the stick he uses is not thicker than his little finger . . ."
—*Judge Tudor Rees.*

Daily Express, Apr. 30th, 1948

Life with the Indomitable British, MAY DAY.

(Snow has fallen in Yorkshire this weekend.)

Sunday Express, May 2nd, 1948

"All right. You despair of the human race, I despair of the human race, we ALL despair of the human race.
Now hold your tongue."

Daily Express, Sept. 10th, 1948

"I gave my son a conjuring outfit for Christmas—what did you give yours?"

Daily Express, Dec. 28th, 1948

"Pedestrian Crossing Week" starts today.

"I have a strong feeling that many English fathers never try to take part in home life. . . . Fathers should learn to bath the baby."—Chairman of the Marriage Guidance Council.
LESSON ONE: FIRST CATCH YOUR BABY.

Daily Express, May 17th, 1949

"You send that in to the *Express* snapshot competition and I'll be handing out the prizes."

Daily Express, July 29th, 1949

"I should have thought we could have managed without your contribution to Mothers' Day."

Sunday Express, Mar. 19th, 1950

"Let's buy Grandma something really useful —like a train-set or some roller skates."

Daily Express, Dec. 12th, 1950

"Dear me, I nearly forgot—we mustn't jay walk now."

Sunday Express, Dec. 12th, 1954

"She says will we please be very careful as it's a trinket set and the one she sent last year got broke."

Sunday Express, Dec. 17th, 1950

"Now you've all decided it's cheaper to go by bus, I suppose I'll have to go by train."

Daily Express, Feb. 27th, 1951

"Do stop mumbling, George. I asked you if anybody called during the week-end."

Daily Express, Aug. 7th, 1951

"As shop steward of this school I warn you that if Churchill gets in he'll have us all making armaments for the bourgeois capitalists' war, which will be a change from plant-stands and trays, anyway."

Daily Express, Sept. 28th, 1951

"They might have told me they were going to build an A-bomb plant opposite *before* they let me buy my own house."

Sunday Express, Dec. 9th, 1951

"We've abominable robins, abominable Santa Clauses at abominable prices—but no snowmen."

Daily Express, Dec. 13th, 1951

"Take your coat out of that puddle, Sir Walter Raleigh—here comes your mum."

Daily Express, Feb. 26th, 1952

"And only last night Dad was saying whatever the Budget result things couldn't get much worse."

Daily Express, Mar. 11th, 1952

"Extra child allowances only encourages 'em—damn phone's going day and night as it is."

Daily Express, Mar. 13th, 1952

"You and your 'Let's sit under that
hedge out of the wind'."

Daily Express, Apr. 7th, 1952

Determination of the British to have their weddings at Easter.

Daily Express, Apr. 12th, 1952

"So you're leaving us because our house is like a rabbit hutch? I did something taking you to see the Stately Homes this Easter, didn't I?"

Daily Express, Apr. 16th, 1952

"Dad—we've found your Cup Final ticket we hid last week."

Daily Express, May 6th, 1952

"I read some interesting facts about education costing more than the police stations, fire stations, libraries, parks and highways all lumped together."

Daily Express, Sept. 1st, 1952

"No, not a Purge—not an S.S. General—not a cosh boy—just Daddy without his keys.
Now be good boys and open the door."

Sunday Express, Jan. 18th, 1953

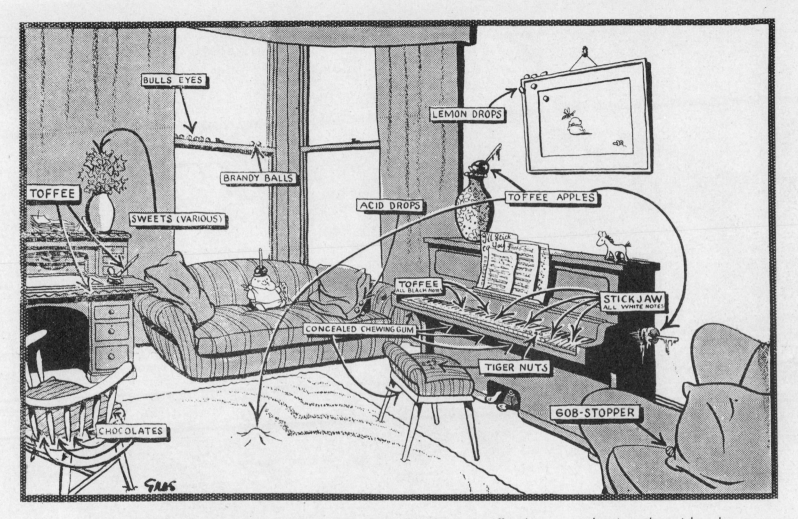

IN THE GILES FAMILY there is a theory among the children that the more toffee they get on the piano the quicker they get their music lessons over—you press one note and they all go down together. I offer this simple sweets-are-now-off-the-ration guide to parents who, during the more or less sweet-free years, may have forgotten the trouble spots.

Daily Express, Feb. 7th, 1953

HOLIDAY CARTOON—Down on the Farm.

Sunday Express, Aug. 16th, 1953

HOLIDAY CARTOON—Now among the soldiers.

Sunday Express, Aug. 23rd, 1953

"While you're up there, Harry—another one wants sixpenn'orth of best softwood cut off that third plank down with 'no notches'. Repeat 'no notches'."

Sunday Express, Nov. 15th, 1953

"Be brave, Miss Loris. Maybe the electricians will call off their strike tomorrow."

Daily Express, Jan. 14th, 1954

"Yes, I know—and I'm STILL putting my plants in."

Daily Express, April 2nd, 1954

"Now, boys, we'll try not to disturb the gentleman while he's painting."

Sunday Express, April 18th, 1954

"Despite the fact that Grandma's corns were giving her what-ho this morning there will be brilliant sunshine everywhere." (Meteorological report.)

Daily Express, June 10th, 1954

"I believe you're glad it's raining so we can't play tennis."

Sunday Express, June 27th, 1954

Dedicated to all those compelled to spend Christmas in hospital, where there is little or no escape from giving a hand with the decorations. I know, I've had some.

Daily Express, Dec. 24th, 1954

"Stand by for squalls.. Somebody is about to connect the empty chicken house with his Christmas dinner."

Daily Express, Dec. 28th, 1954

"We MIGHT be in Regent's Park—he MIGHT have escaped from a circus—and you MIGHT learn to read
a —— map one day, mightn't you, dear?"

Daily Express, Jan. 19th, 1955

"Watch this M.P. pick my brother up—we've painted him all over with treacle."

Sunday Express, April 24th, 1955

"If you take my tip, sir, you'll put a match to it before my sergeant sees it."

Daily Express, June 18th, 1955

"That's a nice thing to say to Grandma when she asked you what our coal stock's like at home."

Sunday Express, July 17th, 1955

"Sergeant, we want reinforcements or extra pay for looking after this lot until someone claims 'em."

Daily Express, Aug. 13th, 1955.

"Go on, Fre

Sunday Exp

him off the lead."

9th, 1955

National Safety Campaign No. 1.

Daily Express, May 31st, 1956

National Safety Campaign No. 2.

Daily Express, June 2nd, 1956

National Safety Campaign No. 3.

Daily Express, June 6th, 1956

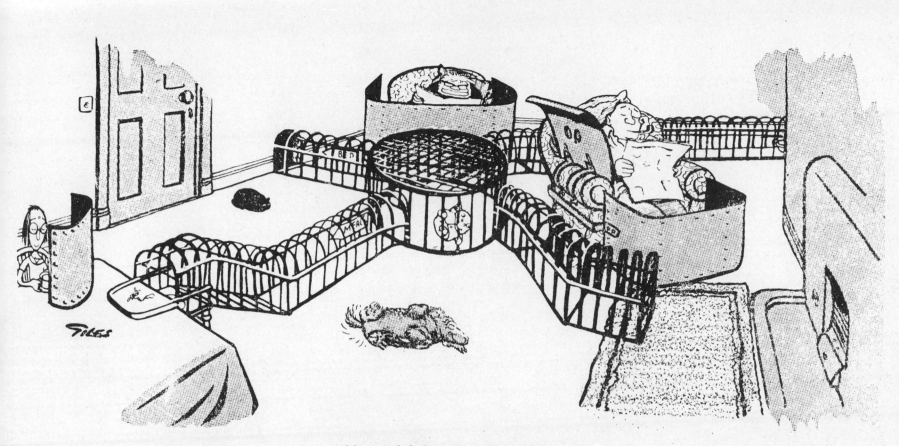

National Safety Campaign No. 4.

Thanks to the great success of the Giles SAFETY IN THE HOME campaign it is now possible to obtain the new "SAFETY-BELT" (*illustrated here*) at all leading stores.

Made of extra-toughened steel, it can be bought in easily assembled sections joined with simple locking nuts, or welded together for good and all time.

The de luxe model is designed to plug into A/C or D/C mains for added protection, and can be supplied lined with barbed wire at slightly extra cost.

Besides keeping your child away from the many danger zones around the house, such as electric points, fires, workshops, pianos, etc., it has the extra advantage of keeping your child away from you. Cats and dogs appreciate this great feature.

The anti-splash barricades shown here are made to withstand heavy peltings from acorns, bread and milk, spanners, marbles, etc., and are worthwhile extras.

Daily Express, June 8th, 1956

"Come home, Father—and we'll promise we won't have Wimbledon on the radio
and television all day long for a fortnight."

Daily Express, June 21st, 1956

"Careful, boys—look where you're going."

Daily Express, Sept. 6th, 1956

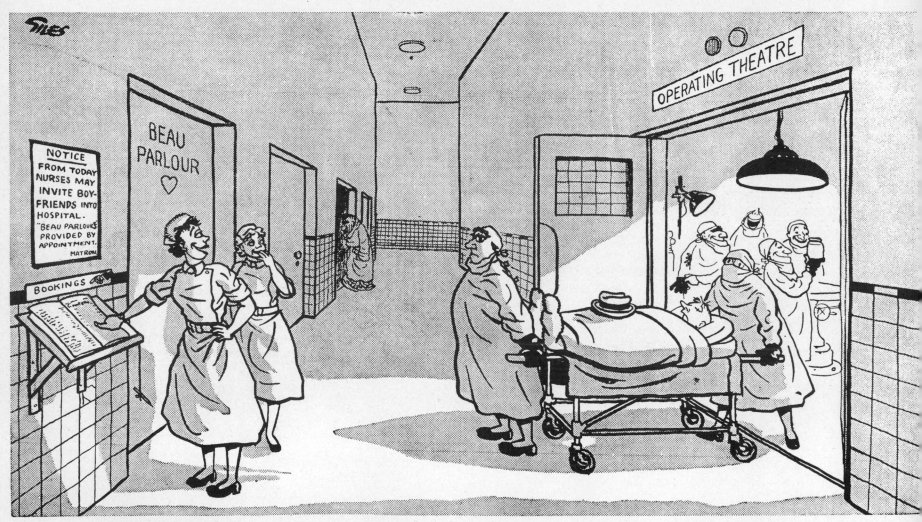

"You've done the wrong one. That's Sister's boy friend—he only called to say 'Good night'."

Daily Express, Oct. 16th, 1956

"Pity we couldn't squeeze another one in—that was my wife."

Daily Express, July 25th, 1957

"I'd show him who's favourite in this house if they ever let him out for a fly round the room."

Sunday Express, Sept. 15th, 1957

DEAR PRINCE PHILIP—With reference to the bit in your speech where you said you were not sure whether farming was a profession or a pastime . . .

Daily Express, November 12th, 1957

"Lady says her electric blanket isn't working."

Daily Express, February 27th, 1958

"Try calling him off again, Tom. This time so he can hear you."

Daily Express, March 27th, 1958

"Polishing rockets on a U.S. base isn't my idea of celebrating the 40th anniversary of the R.A.F."

Daily Express, April 1st, 1958

"Here comes somebody now. Ye gods—I hope that isn't mine."

Daily Express, April 3rd, 1958

"Here we are, litter bugs."

Sunday Express, April 6th, 1958

"Is that you, George? What do you think—a man called and gave me two tickets for 'My Fair Lady'
for your Cup Final ticket."

Daily Express, April 29th, 1958

"I'll bet you didn't notice my L-plates when you thumbed for a lift, sir."

Daily Express, May 6th, 1958

"George! The gentleman you've been giving a lift all week says you promised
to take his family for a Sunday morning spin."

Sunday Express, May 11th, 1958

"Ask vicar if we can have first and last verses only so you can get home for the England v. U.S.S.R. match?
I most certainly will *not*!"

Sunday Express, June 8th, 1958

"Next time you go on strike for seven weeks you want to make sure everybody's off the bus."

Sunday Express, June 22nd, 1958

"Next time you do a Walter Raleigh, use your own coat, not mine."

"Smile, please."

Sunday Express, June 29th, 1958

"How blessed is he who leads a country life, Unvexed with anxious cares, and void of strife!"—DRYDEN (1631–1700).

Daily Express, July 9th, 1958

"I hope that's not my report he's writing—he's smiling."

"Remember—we aren't playing polo, we aren't at the White City, we aren't Wells Fargo.
Just once to the pier and back nice and slow."

Daily Express, July 24th, 1958

"And stop saying ' Ye gods—two whole weeks' in front of the children."

Daily Express, July 29th, 1958

"This'll be a change from listening to her blaring wireless—here comes her husband."

Sunday Express, August 3rd, 1958

"That's the Sherlock Holmes who reported me for dropping a toffee paper on the beat."

Sunday Express, August 10th, 1958

"What's so bright in the news today that you keep chirping 'Goodie, goodie'?"

Daily Express, September 16th, 1953

"I'm working to my own rules, brother—no more 'oola 'oops upstairs or down."

Daily Express, October 3rd, 1958

"Sorry, folks, we can't show you our holiday films and baby's first birthday party—
projector's packed up."

Sunday Express, December 21st, 1958

"If you please, Miss Peeble!"

Daily Express, January 2nd, 1959

"All I want is someone from the B.B.C. programme to come and ask me why we do it."

Sunday Express, January 18th, 1959

"An hour every day to the speed of Moto Perpetuo will take care of some of those extra pounds."

Daily Express, January 22nd, 1959

"Anyone would think *we* let that blessed goal through that put your team out of the Cup."

Sunday Express, February 15th, 1959

"I know what you're trying to do—you're trying to give me a cold so that I part with my Cup replay ticket."

Daily Express, March 3rd, 1959

"When those among us who failed to remember to put their clocks forward are comfortably seated I will continue."

Sunday Express, April 19th, 1959

"If *we'd* learned Latin we'd know what he was saying."

Sunday Express, May 10th, 1959

"I hope I grow tall enough to clip Chalky one across the ear just once before they ban boxing."

"Remember how we laughed at the Joneses for wasting their money going abroad with a lovely summer like this at home?"

Daily Express, July 30th, 1959

"Come now—be brave soldiers—there's no 'arm in an inspection by the new lady M.O."

Daily Express, September 3rd, 1959

"Psst!"

Daily Express, September 10th, 1959

"Frankly, young man, I do NOT recall patting your head in the last election and whispering I'd abolish schools if your father voted for me."

Daily Express, September 24th, 1959